Be

Motivated

(You can do it)

By

EDEN WILSON

Table of contents

Chapter 1

Understanding the concept of motivation

Motivation keeps the human race alive. A person can benefit much from motivation. It can assist someone in achieving their goals or improving themselves. You have the freedom to do whatever you want when it comes to motivation for progress. What motivates you helps you to improve yourself. Due to your willingness to step outside of your comfort zone and try new things, you will ultimately achieve significant personal growth. To reach your objectives and do whatever you want to do, you need motivation. It can aid someone in self-discovery. It may also affect you inside. It is an emotion that will motivate you to work hard from the bottom of your heart. It originates from the part of your heart where you create happiness, success, and all other possibilities.

Self-motivation is the finest form of motivation, however, if you're persistent, individuals may get so inspired that they won't give up. Self-motivation may make you feel incredibly accomplished when you accomplish a goal. When it comes to self-motivation, you are acting only for your own benefit. You are not making a change or setting greater goals for someone else. Selfishly, it's largely because you have to. Usually, punishment is used to inspire people. The best approach to start going isn't usually to start from somewhere. When another person inspires you to give up, they give you an option, and you feel pressured to change, or you will fail because they give you an ultimatum, and this energy brag will not let you quit until you have attained your desired goal. The finest motivation comes from accomplishing something for your own sake which makes you become inspired by other things. Peers can inspire you, but you'll also discover that you have a strong inner drive that will inspire you to pursue your goals. You should consider why someone is trying to encourage you before attempting to discover a technique to motivate yourself.

People now claim that the prospect of financial gain motivates them to labor. Even though you believe that your incentive for working is financial, there is also ego involved. With a little self-motivation, you may achieve your objectives and advance your profession because of all the success you will encounter. Success is a great claim, but you aren't solely driven to work because of the money.

Motivating factors and causes may do a lot for one's ego, self-worth, and sense of completion. They search for motivation throughout their lives, yet the solution is within themselves. People are driven by several factors. Most of the time, people are driven by the need to feel complete...

Chapter 2

How motivation can help to increase your self-esteem

You'll see that motivation affects more than just how you feel; it also affects how you see the world. With motivation, you'll discover the truth that once things start to go your way, you'll feel good about yourself and your life.

These are moments when you'll be able to assess your life objectively and the ability to truly enjoy life is the first method that motivation will boost your self-esteem. Simply said, you'll feel better about yourself and it may boost your confidence.

The ability to choose what and where you want to go next is the second method that motivation will boost your self-esteem. You eventually reach a point where you can accept things as they are. Your outlook on life will alter, and you'll start to strive for greater things. There are various ways to discover motivation, and once you do, you'll be happier overall because you'll realize how many opportunities there are for change. You'll be able to see that you have options and that you can act differently. When you start to have a positive outlook, you can appreciate other people.

Another benefit of motivation is that it will force you to think about topics you may not have previously considered and will motivate you to do so. In order to have a purpose to pursue more in life, you need motivation. You will not be able to succeed in anything until you can change for the better, feel more motivated to put yourself out there and aim for bigger and higher things.

The pursuit of goals in the future is the third method that motivation will boost your self-esteem. This is a terrific way of life because it allows you to start identifying the things that bring you joy. You'll feel more successful in the way you intended, and you'll feel better about everything in your life as well as yourself. You'll start to shift your thoughts from being negative to being optimistic. Due to the fact that you are considering the items you could wish to consider, everything will appear to alter. Things that might inspire confidence in you.

Appreciate the little things in life from the success you will discover in yourself. The ability to motivate oneself to pursue other goals will enable you to succeed in your accomplishments, which makes motivation crucial. Good outlook when everything starts out well and turns out to be the things.

Many activities in life look quite doable without motivation, and you may even feel certain that you can accomplish them. What renders it meaningless is that, when you are motivated, you feel better about yourself because you know what you're capable of accomplishing is worthwhile. When you are driven to do anything, to get you moving, it is a wonderful sensation; however, you simply need to discover the appropriate item to become full of hopefulness. Finding a cause that you can be enthusiastic about is all that is required. Your self-esteem and self-confidence will rise as a result of motivation.

Although you may believe that it is simple to inspire others, you will discover that certain individuals are difficult to inspire, and you may also feel upset because you are unable to do so.

You must first motivate and energize yourself if you want to inspire and energize others. However, you need to have patience when you are eager to push something further because you are thrilled about it.

Even though it could appear to be bribery, you'll discover that many bosses are willing to help others. It might be difficult to inspire oneself to become

aroused soon enough, therefore you must
discover a technique to do it. You'll
discover that life will be difficult. If you're
the coach of a sports team, you'll notice
that when you approach others with a lot
of enthusiasm and energy, they start to
feel the same way.

Another thing to consider would be
rewarded. Rewarding employees, usually
makes them more enthusiastic and
motivated to share your sentiments with
people around you.

To get enthusiastic about something is to
energize others. You'll discover that
about something. You'll be able to share

the delight if you can locate it. When trying to encourage a team, the first thing you should do is offer awards since they will get everyone's heart rate up.

The incentives need not be substantial; in fact, even a little reward will align with Maslow's hierarchy of requirements. You'll discover that your team or employees will receive a lot of support. Another issue is that individuals are more willing to work harder for the good of the group or the organization, which is something to consider. They will start looking forward to a reward as they start to see results from their efforts, and you can then use that information to encourage and reward them.

To positively encourage your athletes or employees, you must let them know that their requirements for self-esteem are being addressed and satisfying wants to make others proud of their work and position inside the organization. It still aids in igniting interest in the job at hand among others. But as a leader or coach, you must set the goals first. You will also need to inspire others.

How significant are you to the business? This is a smart move since it inspires other people. Members will feel inspired and energized when they have their five fundamental needs met, for example, if you tell them what all of their efforts will accomplish Most of the time when you start at a large firm. If your fundamental needs are met, combined with those for safety, relationships, and self-expression they will be highly motivated. You must encourage them to continue working hard and meet their self-esteem requirements. You'll be determined and motivated to complete the theory's self-actualization phase. In this, you'll spend your entire life working to fulfill all of your demands before deciding to improve yourself.

If you can look after your staff or players, you will be able to and you'll see that they'll work more for the team's common objectives. This is the most effective technique to energize and inspire people to be motivated. You two will understand each other and wish to be together. Maslow demonstrates that if you take care of your employees' fundamental needs, they will be motivated and driven to put in a lot of effort toward the group's or company's goals.

attain all of the organization's or group's objectives.

Chapter 3

How motivation will increase your productivity at work

Finding ways to foresee a promotion or starting a new job with the promise of a raise is the key to ensuring that your employment is motivating. You do this so that you have a goal to inspire others to pursue it. The most common problem with most individuals is that they just do not have a career that they believe you may have potential in. This will decrease motivation and cause you to want to make sure that you select a job that will provide you room to improve. These methods may allow you to. If you're going to accept a job that demands a lot of your time and attention, you'll want to be sure that you can devote the necessary time and effort to it. If you're prepared to put in a lot of effort, your employment should appear to be rewarding. This implies that if you are aware of the steps you need to follow, you will be inspired and motivated to finish the work. You'll want to confirm that you discover something in the crucial duties. If they do not have a job at work that they enjoy, you must be willing to fill it.

If you wind up accepting a job that is too much for you to manage, you won't have a job yet feel the need to get another one.

All you need to do is overcome your doubts about your abilities, and you'll discover the will to overcome your workplace fears hindering you. You may be afraid of losing the extra productivity. There is a compelling argument for motivating those who lack the willpower to do the necessary effort. What ought you to do? There must be something that is the first to inspire your motivation.

Believing in oneself is the least you will ever need to do. if you can. The main reason you need to discover motivation is to feel better about your accomplishments if you fight for them rather than merely wanting to wonder why it takes so much effort to get things handed to you. You'll discover that your motive is less important than your motivation. Let's imagine you have the ability, but you are struggling with self-motivation due to some sort of emotional or mental struggle.

You could simply not be prepared for more. You won't feel as though you have to pursue the position of CEO, but that doesn't mean you shouldn't. You could just be concerned with how other people view you. The numbers hold the majority of the significance in production.

If you put in more effort, others will follow suit, and the business will take note of these tiny triumphs and reward you for your efforts.

either by top management or by receiving encouragement from people you like and then sticking with it. Additionally, you must make sure that you must examine yourself to identify a role in your work or profession that you can embrace and that will provide you with a bright future. Increasing your output is the only way to get recognized by your coworkers.

Motivation for employees

There are several ways to inspire someone, but you need to do it if you want to finally increase your output and therefore your profit. With motivated staff, you stand to earn a lot, but you must understand how to do it differently. There are several methods you may use to inspire your staff.

Productivity follows after which you advise them to establish new objectives or offer constructive feedback. Some individuals are perfectionists, and by providing them with constructive criticism, you might inspire them to improve. You may encourage them at this point by praising them in order to inspire them. Their compliments and recommendations are the first method. It's admirable that you want to inspire your employees.

When it comes to encouraging someone, you need to be upbeat and give them a small boost in their self-esteem. The second strategy is to consider the person and their characteristics before attempting to inspire them to keep working toward their objectives. This is how you should behave toward the staff. Since each person is unique, they should all be treated differently.

You are encouraging them to aim higher by putting them on a list of those who may eventually be let go, so they will be more likely to consider the force. Keep yourself from being a bully. If you put forth more effort than before encouragement and comprehension comes both from peers and from inside. Many businesses truly want their employees to improve, therefore you'll want to provide one of the most crucial things you'll need to inspire your team members to care about both their individual ambitions and the company's goals. You must be able to demonstrate to your staff that you genuinely care about their advancement. Then giving

the employees items to inspire them may
be a bad idea if you find that you are
losing patients because of that employee.
performance or goal-setting, or both. The
third technique to inspire a worker is to
have them sit down and have a
conversation with you. If they are aware
that they are being watched, you will
discover via conversation that they will
work more. If they are aware of the best
way to approach the employee going
forward. Motivation is a force that comes
from all over that helps an employee
reach their full potential. It originates
from management, and occasionally nice
awards are given to the staff. The
comments are encouraging for the

workers. You must demonstrate to your staff that both of you are motivated. You'll be able to locate anything with strength or will. Although it is not advised, if nothing else, employees will come to appreciate them if you sometimes offer them gifts.

Rewards will work out if you find that your employees aren't offering you what you require. When negotiations come to a standstill, this may be a little raise, a paid day off, or an additional approach. Once you have exhausted all ethical options, they can give it their all. You can have some support and understanding with a few friendly words.

However, with vacation days, etc., this is a method to start the motivation at work. Just give them a little bit to brag about, then challenge them with a prize. Additionally, you should engage great workers.

Stay motivated at work

Finding a cause to go to work, much less enjoy things that would otherwise depress you, may be quite difficult. After deciding that you're going to have a wonderful day, you should consider eating. To feel refreshed is the first step of the day. For you to be able to work, you must receive at least eight hours of sleep. You may, however, start the day off

with plenty of inspiration and feel rested.
Those that get little to no sleep will only
discover the resolve to enjoy their jobs.
There are many things that might
depress someone during the course of the
day, so don't let the routine of your life
get to you to handle the remainder of the
day.

Additionally, a wonderful and healthy
breakfast will provide you with the
necessary energy. You must be able to let
things go when you wake up. You may
feel inspired to have fun because you
slept plenty. You should consider every
option that the day could hold. The secret
to finding the inspiration for a joyful day

at work is to not let your back, once you have had the appropriate amount of sleep. You can't take your day so seriously.

You must look within for the drive to enjoy oneself. You only need to wake up with the belief that everything is possible. Did you know that? Inspiration to have a cheerful attitude throughout the day If you see that your drive is waning, you might want to consider anything that has the effect of making others laugh when you start your day with the belief that this day is different from all the others. Giving in to these folks is a smart idea. Allow someone to have a nice life in order to have positive karma. Karma is similar to letting go for one's own benefit. Karma is the way that the world treats you, and some individuals find it easier to laugh than grieve. If you don't believe in Karma, though, you could choose to reflect on your own life to find the positive aspects of the day.

People find it simpler to do their jobs when they say, "What comes around, goes around." By interacting with people, you'll discover that by doing a little amount of good for them, you'll ultimately receive something in return from the world. The idea is that, for example, if you pass a homeless person on your way to work, if you mention something recent that you enjoyed and then use it as motivation, it would be helpful. Everyday motivation comes from karma. For individuals who find it difficult to inspire themselves, starting the day on the principle that "good deeds bring good deeds" can help you lead a good life.

Will today turn out to be extraordinary? It is real! Because of Karma, you'll discover that finding the drive to enjoy yourself at work is simpler every day. You'll discover that you'll be able to inspire yourself to work harder and even live a life that makes you delighted to

have a job. Many individuals despise
their jobs, but if you can find the positive
in any situation, you'll be able to live a
happy life and like your work.

Chapter 4

Motivation for a recovering drug addict

The issue with folks attempting drug recovery is that you need to people attempt to maintain their sobriety for a variety of reasons, but they are mostly them. A recovered addict has to desire to continue being sober thereby dropping the ball.

Where in a person does such motivation reside? a certain level of drive to maintain sobriety and steer clear of triggers for your potential sobriety. What motivates you to consider quitting

drinking other from the worry that you
won't have their love and comfort
anymore? There are numerous, but if you
have motivation, you can overcome
anything. You should also become used
to the fact that everyone has a small
amount of incentive inside of them, in
which they may use to motivate
themselves to keep themselves clean.
People clean up so that they can maintain
their comfort.

However, if you can simply discover that
most of the motivation that an addict in
recovery requires comes from within
their own life. There are a lot more

reasons to discover the drive to accept the truth; this is only one of them.

This indicates that you are unable to conceal yourself behind drug-induced feelings. You cannot continue to use drugs. You might also fully commit to a task. Finding something you enjoy doing can help you stay motivated during your recuperation. Learning to paint, sketch, write, play, or engage in any other activity that enables you to accept failure without giving into self-pity is a great way to discover inspiration which will drive you'll need to succeed, due to the fact that they have a firm hold on life and reality, a great many people are able to maintain sobriety.

You will discover that there is life when you choose these things over drugs. The drugs are in command, but if you have enough drive, you can shift your attention away from your dependence on them. When you use drugs, you are not in control of yourself or your family, who you can rely on for the support you need to discover the drive to stop. You should be able to go through the challenging times and return from rehab. You may rely on your friends for encouragement to embrace who you are and the bravery to change rather than allow yourself to feel sorry for themselves. It will get much simpler over time since they are driven to get up. You won't experience as many cravings, and you'll be able to reach out for real life rather than narcotics.

Many artists grow a secret skill that they may rely on until they are prepared to stand on their own. When you become addicted to drugs, it is difficult to clean up after yourself and you may use it as a crutch for years.

Like an artist, you'll draw inspiration from the connection to your work.

It can be someone else, but it needn't be. If you can rely on a close family member or loved one until you are ready to stand on your own, long after you have been dependent on drugs. Because of this, you need to locate something in a painting that will keep you inspired.

What kind of addictions you have is irrelevant. The only thing that counts is you, and that's what will keep you from turning back to your addictions.

In actuality, the majority of people who struggle with recovery end up needing the help of others in order to succeed in breaking free from their addiction. Make sure this is something you desire for yourself most of all.

Having the courage to say "No" is the hardest step. The next phase is more challenging. that you are eager to discover solutions to them. You must discover your own motivation, which you will do by looking within. If you go off the wagon, your impact on their addictions will be greater than ever. If you believe that you must give up for yourself, you won't ever give up. Just take a moment to unwind and find something within to ensure that you're doing it because you want to, not because you feel like it Before you decide to resign, you must have both the proper incentive and internal motivation, otherwise, you will never succeed. compelled or under pressure to perform. You will start to find additional motivation to help you desire to heal if you are truly devoted to your rehabilitation. You must always say no in the second stage.

You must start to rely on some of the things that inspire you to maintain your sobriety in order to find the restraints you will need. Your sober and clean friends, family, and hobbies may all play a significant role in your recovery, but there are also a lot of other things that you need to be open to in order to fully heal.

Everyone struggles to stay sober and clean, but certain addictions need learning how to identify what motivates you so that you don't experience cravings or the addiction itself. Motivation may originate from a wide variety of items and/or activities in which you may find interest. Once you discover the drive to stop the detrimental activity, do so. You'll become stronger if you do anything else instead of engaging in addictions. You could wish to ponder and feel driven to create a clean and sober existence for yourself once you are able to understand life and truth.

There are other things like sex, the internet, and gambling addictions that the need to return to the gambling or

whatever your addiction may be once you
discover a tiny amount of drive that
prevents you from the addiction.
avoid using drugs.

There are several items that can save you
from ruining your life. There may be an
issue. In these circumstances, you will
draw strength from those close to you
and may decide to seek the assistance of
a therapist to help you deal with the
additional needs.

Things that will help you to maintain
your sobriety and keep others away from
you are given to you in support of your
recovery.

the most when you feel the need to err, but by utilizing the inspiration you receive from others and yourself, you should be able to recover inspiration from others and be affected by the supportive reactions that people around you provide.

You will find the power to overcome addictive habits and the bravery to do so if you discover how to and stick with your recovery from friends and family's support. You'll require support without any slip-outs.

Chapter 5

How you can motivate yourself

You'll discover that it is most difficult to motivate oneself. If only you knew how fantastic it feels to inspire yourself. You might be able to discuss your feelings with someone close to you, and they will assist you. You may unblock all of your channels and discover things to do if you'd want to find a method to assist in the manner that you work on yourself. Simply said, it is so much simpler to share your ideas with people than it is to consider getting counseling if you feel bad about yourself.

There are a plethora of additional methods you might inspire yourself. You'll possess

Respecting who you are and accepting who you are are both necessary. Finding a good, solid self-esteem, strong, solid strategy to approach your lack of motivation is the key to inspiring yourself. When you are capable, you will have the actual drive to pursue your goals, unlike others who just lack inspiration to discover the things you truly find fascinating. People are everywhere. Speaking with someone about your feelings is not a terrible idea; in fact, it may be a good way to give yourself some guidance. It's difficult to stimulate someone's eye so they are driven to pursue it further, regardless of whether you are the sort who can be readily motivated or not.

The majority of individuals merely require that extra push, but other people need more.
Make sure you are on the proper route to stay on it in order to maintain your motivation. You don't want to be simply like everyone else. You must learn how to inspire yourself and stop caring about external motivation. These people are never happy since self-motivation is believing in your own abilities rather than constantly depending on others for

approval. The negativity that arises is not something you can listen to. You should be aware that you won't be able to accomplish everything since they are always pursuing the ambitions of other people. You cannot, however, let other people's opinions derail your motivation if you find the skill you desire. regarding others If it's something you really want to happen in one night, it doesn't matter what the others are. To find the items, you will need to put in a lot of effort.

The worst thing about folks who lack motivation is that they have lives that you really want to live, forcing you to take action.

the greatest concepts and creations known to man. who need a shove into reality is the focus. They require the assistance of others to motivate them to act. Even the most outlandish things turn out to be the finest way to self-motivate people discover the best type of happiness because they stay grounded and maintain their optimistic outlook. You must always turn a negative into a positive when you hear something.

That includes any negativity you might experience as a result of falling short of your own expectations. You'll discover that being able to accomplish your own goals allows you to be truly satisfied. You will find the drive to maintain your aspirations, though, if you can learn to muster the fortitude to keep trying.

The most difficult thing you will ever have to do is motivate yourself, but when you succeed and can see for yourself that you have achieved your objective, it will all have been worth it.

Chapter 6

How you can motivate others

You may believe that inspiring people is simple, yet success depends on how well your message is received. The first thing you should do is remove the pronoun "you" from your sentences. However, if you want to inspire someone, you could be just the one to do it. Consider your approach, your tone of voice, and how you say things since you might need to put yourself on the defensive. You'll discover that others are going to say the same thing. You need to be able to communicate effectively so that nothing goes wrong and everything turns out as it should. Find something your loved one is genuinely enthusiastic about.

When you consider how you seem to others, both via your actions and the language you employ. Regarding communication style, both your own and mine. You might not be the kind of person who can say things like, "I think you," but you'll discover that people want you to think things out before you say them.

You ought to possess the ability to inspire others. When individuals don't know that what they are saying could not be true, you'll want to remove all of the unfavorable criticism from your motivating speech.

Putting someone down will not inspire them. You can't strive to leave for something greater and larger. If you are used to doing all the communicating, it might be quite difficult to just be a friend to them. But you want him or her to discover something. This is crucial because you must learn to listen instead of attempting to inspire others. forcing someone to move while listening to them. That just is not how things operate. You'll find that you may effectively reinforce any message you want to convey to a person.

This is crucial because they will be inspired by your encouragement to misunderstand your intentions in light of the circumstances. You must inspire someone by showing them that you care about them and are there for them whenever they need you.

ask yourself why it's important individual, you will ultimately realize that you will urge them to be a better because you want the best for them, not because of what you lack in yourself. are going to need to learn how to or you will never be able to truly some motivation.

Before you go, try approaching someone and asking them to help you discover your life. You must be careful with the words you use and the manner you pronounce them.

However, in order for you to fully comprehend the image and who you are. Anyone can be difficult to inspire. Simply being a human is all that is required. How to motivate someone is subject to a number of restrictions.

To start a better and closer relationship with someone and assist them in finding the proper path, all you have to do is be there for them as a support system and keep them in your thoughts in order for them to discover something that inspires them.

Anyone who can be a good friend may inspire someone to aim higher and accomplish more. Anyone who can be a good friend can keep the channels of communication open. Additionally, you should continually coming up with fresh suggestions to encourage others to go higher.

Chapter 7

Stay motivated by saving money

You are aware of what encourages individuals to make savings. Fear: fear aids with productivity. You might get injured in the end. You must confirm your capability.

You will discover that a safety net has a significant chance to lose everything. If you don't learn how, you'll wind up losing a lot since you never know when anything could happen. You risk losing your incentive to develop a saving habit since it helps individuals understand their potential and how motivating it is to have a safety net. Because you never know when the tough times may come, you'll want to make sure that you locate the drive as soon as possible. In life, you will discover. You may be better off if you learn to save money incrementally since you never know what may occur. It's crucial to manage your finances and save money. Don't wait until something has already occurred, like having your car towed.

ability to wind up with a sizable chunk of change. It's crucial to save money so that you can take care of yourself.

Several other ideas that may cross your mind when searching

You may wish to put money aside with the intention of taking a trip; this means that your goal is not to have it for a rainy day.

put away for later. The more you genuinely want something, the more you will realize that there is never enough money for the future.

This is a terrific reason to save some money since you will love yourself in motivation for saving money is something that you always desired. You will consider how much money it will cost to make the. perhaps buy a vehicle, a house, or anything else substantial and meaningful

Being unable to work and having no means of support once you retire is a frightening situation. People from the baby boomer generation who are currently concerned about normal behavior generally wouldn't buy if conserving money for anything specific is not what you want to do.

You will need to work hard to save the money after making the purchase. how they intend to survive. They are concerned about how things will turn out. You'll have experience working hard for something, and you can decide to keep the money for the future. There are several reasons to consider your future plans constantly. The more you are able to save, the better off you will be able to live.

Another reason to save is to ensure that the unplanned expenses are covered. This will give you more time to concentrate on the things that require a decision, and it will also give you peace of mind.
If you save money for your future, those terrible occurrences will help to offset any losses you may incur. You will discover that a lot of things are going to happen, but use the time to focus on the things that matter to you most and stop feeling sorry for yourself.

rather than your financial difficulties.
There will be lots of things available to
you. Maybe one day you'll find yourself at
a fork in the path. You're moving like
cash.

Chapter 8
Building a Spirit of Teamwork

When faced with an evolving scenario involving a group of individuals, you'll discover that everyone will appreciate the guidance and come to understand what has to be done to bring the group together, but as a team.

However, if you maintain the lines of communication open, you can always learn how to become a great leader by attending some workshops and seminars. If you see that the group has gotten off track from a task, you will also need to learn how to operate as a team and

inspire the group's boss. when you join
the group as the leader.

One of the finest ways to inspire a team is
to recognize that it need some leadership
and direction.

an organization that has leadership but
not absolute power. Avoid seeming
arrogant.

The ability to come and be a great
communicator and listener is another
thing you might want to keep in mind.
Additionally, you should be honest; there
is no reason why you cannot provide
some of your own suggestions. To
collaborate with one another. You are
bringing strong leadership abilities to the

group in many many ways. Bring the group back through varied activities that will motivate them. Leadership qualities are difficult to acquire.

Some of these things can include taking a brief pause, going over the
If you search up certain task-oriented hobbies, you'll also discover that communication is encouraged.

If you truly want to inspire someone, you must find it within yourself to be able to lead the group's course and maintain control of your own actions since it depends on the people with whom you are interacting. You may even inspire anyone by asking the group to come up with a solution.

You may choose from a variety of activities, and you can get lots of inspiration online or from more senior coworkers. You'll discover that you may do it within the team as well. Your ability to motivate your team will depend on your ability to communicate, but you should constantly consider the sort of team you are on and the people you are working with.

Being a team member teaches you many valuable life lessons. You'll learn even more about the channels of communication and how to communicate effectively to persuade the team to agree with you and to give you the motivation you need to keep the team energised and prepared for the tasks at hand. Keep your attention on the task at hand. It is crucial that you develop your leadership skills since if you are a competent leader, your team won't be under your control. Additionally, if you are teaching a group of people, you should think of task-oriented exercises that will help the group work as a unit.

As a leader, you'll discover that it's crucial for you to be able to absorb everything with a positive outlook. Keep in mind that you will be a member of a positive team if you are a good leader. Give it the time and effort necessary to learn how to communicate properly, encourage people, and manage teams so that you may get leadership experience. Being a leader is an honor, and the team you build is what your team needs to survive. If you don't, the squad will fall short.

Chapter 9

Be motivated in your marriage

The way you kiss you and the way you light up a room are both motivating factors when it comes to marriage. All of these individuals should rank among your closest friends and family members.

There are several factors that will encourage you to get married and maintain your marriage. Even if the issues are commonplace and straightforward, it is the little things that make or break a relationship.
First, the things that will pursue you to marry or stay things like the way they

look at you, examples of motivation that someone gives to their partner when it comes to could be something as simple as a smile that could convince one to get married, are what motivate you to get married and to stay married. This individual will be with this person. This guy will do so many actions that your own emotions would be the second.

The second motivating factor for getting married or staying in an unhappy marriage. A day scared that you won't see them again, you know that it is love, and that it is just right. However, you should also be aware that there will be other elements at play. You'll discover that love is strangely compelling. If you believe you could love someone indefinitely, it is. one decision upon waking.

The main factor that will influence your decision to get married or engage in a procedure is the one that will most likely motivate you. However, you could discover that your family or friends will combine these groups to push you to get married. Family and friends are typically the first to see our own uncertainties when it comes to matters like those. Your sentiments for your spouse and all the little things are what make a marriage. If you let them have a significant influence on your life, such as your marriage, they will be leading it. Because everything will seem to be unpleasant or beautiful, we allow ourselves to be inspired by other people. There will be instances when you should either support or reject the thoughts you have about when the time is right and when it isn't. You'll see that however we tend to let other people influence our decision-making, it will have a significant effect on our emotions and hearts. When you are uncertain, you will experience it, but everyone does.

Chapter 10

Be clean

If you need encouragement to be clean, then something is very wrong with you. You will be evaluated based on your looks, even if you give off the appropriate impression. Impressions are crucial, but you should also maintain a professional demeanor if you don't want to face discrimination due to how you treat your coworkers. Take a look around to see how your area compares to others. It may be you, your house, your automobile, or even your place of employment.

It wouldn't be a good idea to leave your workspace in disarray either. In fact, maintaining cleanliness could be necessary for employment. You ought to show either. People will undoubtedly think you and your job are slobs, as you will discover.

Being tidy and clean is something you should strive for since it speaks well of you.

Everything you do and don't do has an impact on who or what you are. You'll be expressing to your coworkers that you just don't care any more. Your outward look will reveal a lot about your character and personality. In order to discover the

motivation when it comes to your
workstation, it is crucial that you go
above and beyond. You may be in your
person.

Unkempt people frequently acquire the
reputation of being filthy and invite
others over to witness it. You'll notice the
contrast between an unorganized house
and, let's say, the entire globe. They are
the ones who are organized and make
others wonder if they are homeless. Most
certainly not, thus you should use it as
inspiration to improve. Additionally, you
may get items cleaned. If your workplace
is well-kept, your employer will feel

happier and more upbeat. Your confidence level will increase.

Additionally, you have to make an effort to maintain a spotless house for the benefit of your single neighbors. You'll discover that folks that appear disheveled do not necessarily suffer from depression, which is another reason to keep your home tidy. They could even believe you to be homeless. Do you really want to be wounded and lonely as a result of all the unpleasant remarks that individuals may make while they work together to locate the ideal career and partner? If they exist, nothing can inspire you.

When looking for a date, being single is not ideal. You'll experience depression even if you succeed. You don't necessarily get a lot of dates on Saturday night because of your hygiene. In fact, they frequently get lonesome. Finding the will to maintain your cleanliness and order at home is crucial. You'll discover that if your flat is disorganized, you'll not only get what you want, but other people won't respect you as much. You may gain the respect you need from people when you look beautiful and smell great.

It's not that difficult to get inspired to live clean. There are a lot of factors. Nobody needs or wants the kind of unfavorable attention that you receive. The main reason for motivation, nevertheless, is to stay away from difficulties. Once you stop being unclean. If you are dirty and unkempt, others will focus on that and it will hinder your ability to advance in life. Being clean has many good effects on life. Being sober paves the way for personal achievement.

Chapter 11

Healthy eating habits

You should consider oneself while seeking inspiration for good eating practices. Obesity affects a huge number of individuals worldwide and might prevent you from being healthy. Numerous factors might motivate someone to begin.

To achieve self control is to find the drive to spend the money on nutritious meals. You will undoubtedly notice a difference in the nutritious foods if you are a grazer putting money aside. You could believe that you are getting greater value for your money, but if you choose a new way of living, you will undoubtedly have the funds necessary because your changing eating patterns will prevent you from experiencing many things and increase the cost of food. The fact is that healthy meals do cost more, but if you eat well, there are numerous factors that prevent you from eating as much as you would like to. However, it is difficult in life for individuals who are morbidly obese if you can muster the strength to start, even though you aren't. You intend to lose weight. Learning to avoid all the sweets and fast food can help you develop a healthy eating habit, which is the first reason why individuals struggle to be motivated to eat well.

The leading causes of healthy eating discouragement include heart disease, stroke, and high blood pressure. You'll discover that you need to eat well for them. When you finally take the time to look within, depression might prevent you from accomplishing some of the things that you would otherwise like to do.

You should make eating nutritious meals a habit since it demonstrates to your family especially your children how to live a fulfilling life. Second, ordinary people take things for granted. Because of all the junk food, there are so many things you may miss. Once more, it does affect how you feel and appear. Even while junk food may taste nice, you'll find that it might make you feel down. Long-term consumption of unhealthy meals will also cause your heart to weaken.

When you don't like the way you appear, you'll get depressed and stop worrying about having low self-esteem. Regarding the family, they are concerned about your health as well as their own. Because you despise yourself, you will be always exhausted and your moods will fluctuate;

but, if you start eating healthily today, you will because of problems affecting you and your family, you can be putting them at risk. You need to put yourself first. You ought to be concerned about missing because you neglected your own needs. You'll discover that you need to start eating healthily since certain meals might be fatal. You are not eating properly after. Because you chose to consume poor meals instead of good foods when you had the option, you will miss a lot of things. Always keep in mind that while eating, you should consider your future. If you require inspiration because of your disregard for your health, the future may see you badly harming

both yourself and others. If you don't
take care of yourself, can you picture
what may happen to you later?
of a health-related nature. In reality, you
could pass away in the future since being
healthy is a decision we should all make,
no matter what.

Chapter 12

Stay motivated as a coach

You will exercise leadership in situations when you are in a position of authority. You must learn how to successfully listen to others before you can start to assume greater leadership duties. You should learn new talents as soon as you can. As the coach, there are a lot of things you can do to inspire the team, but first you need to own up to some mistakes. In order to be an effective coach, you must first locate the drive within yourself.

Your ability to express yourself effectively will enable people to understand your thoughts as well as the manner in which you may demonstrate your leadership. The ability to inform people that you are prepared for such a position is necessary, but coaching entails more than that.

It's incredibly easy to boost your motivation and become a coach. You can take on extra responsibility by requesting a leadership position. You will discover that this is the case since, in addition to learning some difficult life lessons, you also want to make the most of it. If you can be a competent leader without being a tyrant, you might be able to lead every day at work. You should aim to get the most out of it.

If you use the lessons you've learned from being a proactive leader, you'll be able to individually inspire people to achieve greater and better objectives since everyone will be inspired in the same manner. When you take the time to speak things out, you may sometimes instruct someone on how to learn or get motivated. Everything will be structured, and there will be a strong support system. When you are the coach, you must give your entire self to the squad. You must develop the ability to inspire your team.

When it comes to inspiring your players, you'll see that many of them are unaware that as a coach, you must provide the squad with direction. This will help you become a better coach. Talk to each player you need to have an individual conversation. You should then take the time to listen to them after asking them about any worries you may have. When dealing with your players, you sometimes need to be firm and other times you need to be compassionate. It's easier when you can spend one-on-one time with your athlete, since you can

Take someone aside and have a serious conversation with them; by doing so, you

can learn how to motivate them and become a coach. Even though you might be eager to become a coach, you can't give up on a player without also giving up on the squad.
for the team and for themselves. Additionally, this is where you'll find the drive to become a coach. But not everyone has what it takes, so you should give everything a go before giving up. In actuality, you really shouldn't ever suggest ways to a coach.

The greatest place for you to discover the drive to lead your team or the drive you really need to be a coach or leader is in the players. They will make you a better leader and coach. The only other is that you'll feel better about who you are. In such a situation, all the motivation will be easy to discover. That will encourage you to accept leadership positions since you'll feel that you need to develop yourself to be a successful leader. By honing your communication abilities, you'll get knowledge from your coach. Your ability to communicate will help you become a better person.

Chapter 13

Building yourself to be motivated

Many people will passively increase their drive in social or professional settings. This implies that you develop motivation without consciously attempting. They do so because they enjoy listening to you. In reality, you'll discover that people will pay attention when you utilize your influence to inspire them.

Your coworkers will respect you and pay attention to you in return.

Your personality will show out in the way that people just

Sometimes it just comes from your inherent nature, and other

When you have power, you can influence people without actively doing anything.

Make sure others are aware of the several forms of authority you might have over someone. There are various ways that you might generate motivation without even realizing it, and others may think that you just possess the necessary talents.
control over them due to your ability to exert influence over all of your subject-specific knowledge.
a pioneer.

If you take the time to actively get to know some of them, you'll discover that they'll start to trust your judgment since they've become accustomed to it.

When you are present, they will be more likely to become motivated.
If you have provided someone a solid foundation of a pleasant connection, even if you don't actually have genuine power over them, you may still have knowledge of them. There are various distinct sorts of authority, and you'll discover that each one may inspire people to work harder to achieve the corporate or group objectives.
Due of their extensive knowledge, subjects frequently have a strong influence.

Additionally, you'll see that your authority may inspire others. authority. Do you not always act quickly when someone asks you to do something since you know so much about it and have influence on them? That is the power of authority; nevertheless, in order to use it, one must be endowed with a powerful personality. For those who can claim to be masters or theorists of a personality, motive plays a significant role. If you lack the ability to compel people to listen, you cannot inspire them. They don't you. Here is when you actually have control over them and may direct them on how to behave or perform at work. You'll be able to inspire some of the individuals you meet through a connection when they are your boss. you with appreciation for your inspiration and drive. You may. Just because you are ranked higher than someone else may allow you to inspire them. You'll discover that if you have an advantage over someone, they will be inspired by you and be motivated.

The next approach to inspire someone is by doing it. You can inspire disappointment in you. These kinds of emotions may be quite powerful, and the drive anytime you have the ability to inspire someone, you should.

This power might inspire someone since they don't want to be around individuals who think they are important or cruel to others. Some individuals will turn to you for guidance and acceptance if you have that kind of relationship with them. They were never able to inspire others. Motivation is a really potent weapon, and getting someone to like you whether on a friendship or romantic level can make it much more potent.

be content with the knowledge that you can inspire someone. Since they aren't many, they should be utilized with care. Additionally, make an effort to influence

someone for their own benefit, not your
own.

Chapter 14

How to motivate others

It may be incredibly challenging and irritating to motivate people. Being able to comprehend one another can help to strengthen your relationship. Once there were some folks who required more inspiration. By aiming for new and greater things, you might find inspiration. Regarding having an open

Additionally, you should consider how you connect with the
No matter if they are friends or relatives, you will discover that a strong connection involves listening to them. Not only

should you pay attention to what people are saying, but you should also communicate with an open mind. You need to be able to comprehend what they are saying. You must be direct and encouraging. In order to inspire one another, you will also need to have respect and understanding for one another.

There are many individuals that may be inspired easily if you have open contact with them and provide them with the support they require. After that, you can consider all of the things you would like to say to the person. The message will also be more apparent if you choose your words carefully before you speak. To encourage someone, you must first come to them with an idea.

There are a number of strategies you may use to inspire people.
You'll need to both demonstrate and convey to them your willingness to offer assistance in any situation. When kids get enthusiastic about something, you need to support and motivate them to pursue it. You don't want to hold them back from getting to where they are. This implies that you need to be aware of their location. You'll want to be supportive of them in your interactions with them.

As you speak, another person may start speaking. Instead of making snap judgments, they wait their turn to instruct the other person. talk when you encourage. You need to have incentive or limit them in addition to being a skilled communicator. To support someone does not imply that you agree with them. You must improve your communication skills. A competent communicator will be able to listen to and comprehend what others are saying when you offer them broad instructions and let them take from them. The next step is to sit down and discuss your motivation with the other individual. You will be talking to them once you can defend yourself. This implies that in order to get your point over properly and have patience, you must explain why you want them to have certain talents. This means that you must give the other person the space to express yourself fully.

However, you must take a critical eye and refrain from being irate or irritated at this time. There are many people who struggle to inspire others. To avoid offending anyone's sentiments, you can find things carefully and objectively you should be able to inspire them and solidify your relationship by getting your point through.

sounding arrogant and partisan. You must be careful while choosing your words, especially when it comes to motivation. It can be frustrating to chat with someone, but if you take the time to get to know them, you will realize that it is necessary to speak your thoughts and pick your words wisely. Otherwise, you risk ending up ending a connection should be able to inspire them effectively. Your connection might get stronger with or without motivation.

Chapter 15

How to be motivated as an artist

Finding inspiration may be challenging for artists. People who lose just show up. The best course of action to take if you don't have enough. The act of writing on paper with a pencil or pen is only one of the numerous activities that will stimulate your creativity.
You are able to locate the inspiration for your inspiration, the drive to start the creative juices flowing.

Art will come to life when there is motivation. How can you get yourself to make something amusing, artistic, and leave it on the floor? Just write without thinking about what you will write with a pencil.

Letting go will be the first thing you must do. Toss a piece of paper upon works of art? as a result of a lack of inspiration, they lack originality. You can use phrases, merely words, or ramble when writing. You might not be able to create on your own if you let yourself. You can find some ideas by writing without thinking sometimes. Around a minute later, you sometimes doesn't function.

You should now venture outside and take a stroll. Don't put too much stock in the

motivation you can find in daily life.
Inspiration for your nieces or nephews to
enjoy themselves at a theme park. You
may enjoy yourself while producing your
piece of art with the straightforward
enjoyment. For people who enjoy
socializing and returning to a
straightforward way of life.
You'll be able to motivate yourself to go
away from it all.
Moreover, art is rare. You may already
have too many, which is the issue.

The seemingly little things all around you
may be so inspiring. If you are a painter
or a drawer, you will get the inspiration

and drive you need by being inspired and motivated to make entertaining art.

You discover that having fun with people helps you release all of your tension, produce beautiful work, and enjoy yourself while doing it.

For enjoyment on your own. You must go outside and engage in some basic entertainment. leave by. If you can, authors will discover that it's difficult to have fun while trying to produce when they have too much on their minds.

However, if we take the time to have art, life becomes more difficult as we get older. You'll discover that if you set aside some time each day to focus on If you're attempting to make something amusing, you might want to go brainstorm some ideas before combining them together. discussing anything, but simply take some buddies to a pub and sit in a park or close to a tree and watch life go by while you release all your tension. When you have some silly time and some basic enjoyment, life doesn't seem that horrible.

It's beneficial to occasionally behave like a child since enjoyment has a positive effect on one's soul and the more fun one has, the more thoughts are perpetually generated in one's head. You'll be motivated and inspired by fun to create something amazing.

You'll be able to draw inspiration for your artistic endeavors from a memory of your carefree youth. Additionally, you'll have a greater sense of self and professional aptitude.

Additionally, people who can utilize fun as inspiration or incentive will have fuller lives. If you manage to locate the items that return you to a better life,

Chapter 16

How motivation and music interact

We derive motivation from a variety of sources when it comes to behavior. peer group,

The problem about music is that it permeates every aspect of life. The lyrics and melody of a song might make you feel something while you listen to it. You'll discover that song contains identical words to another, but a totally distinct sound. Some individuals use music as a source of motivation, either positively or negatively, to locate you. Music has a way of inspiring people from a very young age.

You can get ready for bed, get amped for a game, or even create some energy. Music has the power to persuade people to act.

Even the lyrics and musical notes of a song might bring you solace.

The point is, you may be motivated by your pet, a movie, or even music. Your mood can change significantly to music. Depending on the music you can purchase

The issue with music is that it has the power to move you. You may connect with the musical aspect of life. Nothing else compares to music's ability to inspire and drive others to follow their aspirations. It moves you forward.

Anything may offer you a positive or even inspire you to start down the correct path depending on how you interpret it. Why and how can music help us overcome challenging situations like drug or alcohol abuse? From a song, the music is better person.
appear to be so strong? Because it may be anything and allows listeners to empathize, music has power. It induces the feeling of unity.

You could feel inspired to tell someone you adore them. A person may be touched by you in such a way that they are motivated to change inside of you. You'll see that your mood will change for the worst or that we may identify with. They are going through something that we might be able to relate to, and they've resolved to turn their lives around.

You can't listen to the radio every day and not recognize your uneasiness and try to see things more positively. Sometimes, you have bad thoughts about yourself or your life. You can be inspired to play a significant role. It gives the impression that there are people who understand change. The power of music inspires courage.

Music becomes progressively more significant to us as we become older. Teenager is inspired to take action. You may listen to music and feel something for years; it helps people find their own identities. Because of a song, an adolescent is able to become more optimistic.

When completely absorbed, music has stronger influence over our ideas and Have you ever observed that you put in longer and harder effort when you start to daydream or daydream? Additionally, music stimulates the blood flow since it inspires. It is evident that it does help you achieve your goals and will keep you motivated. It could have a radio on. People have been shown to work more diligently when music is present than when it is not. That is why a lot of companies and institutions play music for their employees. Why individuals feel differently from what your parents or partner could have is not entirely known. There is something about the beat of music that motivates you to work harder. inspires others to work harder. Music is energy, if there is anything. It will just serve as a way to break the awkward quiet, but it

Music always serves as inspiration. You'll discover that music gets you moving and might motivate you to improve yourself.

Chapter 17

Motivation resources

Are you seeking for self-improvement books? Are you aware that it may be done offline or online. Are there any places right now where you can find inspiring books? Not only may you buy a the book store, you'll want to stop by the desk clerk and inquire where the self-help or motivational books are placed. You can also buy these books at any nearby book store. Then, once you arrive, you may visit any nearby malls or book stores to locate anything or learn how to pick up a new interest.

You might want to be more explicit about what you're seeking for when searching for a cookbook or a self-improvement book. You may require. You may discover a book to inspire you for anything. If you don't want to buy the book, you may check it out from the library. You can find the motivating books you're seeking for if you're wanting to buy any. However, there are a ton of books about motivation available online through different websites. Additionally, you may get a motivational book at the bookstore. Browse the selection to see which titles are perfect for you.

Additionally, since books are often rather expensive, you may want to seek for advice or guidance.

There are numerous choices, but you may discover thousands of inspirational books on these shelves. You may order the book online and have it delivered to your home, or you

The nicest thing about buying a book online is that you may select from a variety of websites that provide books. You should make sure to read a few pages of the book. webpages resembling those of Barnes & Noble also consider the review. You'll be able to do this while still enjoying your own company and finding the ideal book for you. You can come and

go from your neighborhood Barns &
Noble to pick up the book as needed, but
you'll find that ordering the book is more
practical for you. Now books stores
employees with inspiration. You can
browse the book at your own pace.

Furthermore, you want to confirm that it
is exactly what you're searching for since;
If you have the time to research anything
online, you might want to because, both
of them will have used copies of the book,
you may decide on your pricing without
feeling pressured to buy it right away.
Amazon.com can also assist you in
finding the book you're searching for.
The may be highly expensive. You will

discover that there are many books that you will add to your collection, and you may get to the new books, and you get to pick the book. There comes a time when you just don't want another book lying around, but some shops don't provide that option.

People visit the library because of this. Because you are not paying for the books, you are free to utilize the library in any way you see fit. Many libraries will send books from other libraries if they don't already have them in their collections. Using monies to utilize money is good. As long as a library is used, the government will continue to support the facilities (local and library services will eventually turn the library and the community into a state).